Norwich in 1880

In the late 19th century, Norwich was an important manufacturing and trading centre and, with its magnificent Cathedral and Castle, was a popular destination for visitors. Detailed guide-books were available to help them make the most of their stay and this booklet combines text from the 'Tourists' Guide to Norfolk' by Walter Rye, published in 1880, with historical photographs from the Keasbury-Gordon Photograph Archive.

It is in three parts. The first is eighteen photographs, probably taken between the 1890s and 1930s; the second, a detailed visitor's guide to Norwich and the third, a fascinating history and general description of Norfolk.

The text and the photographs complement each other and enable us to travel back in time to visit this important British city over one hundred years ago. I hope you enjoy the journey.

Andrew Gill

Celebrating Queen Victoria's Jubilee

Orford Place

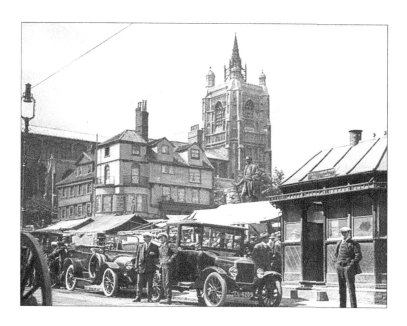

Market Place

Prince of Wales Road

Norfolk wherries leaving for the Broads

After the Colegate Street flood

Queue for the fish and chip shop

The Cathedral from Rosary Road

The Guildhall

Market Place

Market Place

Norfolk Wherries

Prince of Wales Road

St. George Street, 27th August, 1912

Tombland

Norwich Golf Club

Bishop's Bridge

The Cock Inn

NORWICH.

As it will, for many reasons, be convenient for us to take Norwich as the starting-point of most of our operations, it will be well, before proceeding to describe that city, to say a few words as to its history. Setting aside conjecture, then, we know that it was known as Caer Gwent before the Romans, who certainly had a Roman settlement here, as we know from the quantity of their coins, and other things belonging to them, which have been found near the Castle and elsewhere. That this was known as Venta Icenorum seems almost as certain, as also that its name of Nord-wic points by way of contra-distinction to the more southerly castle of Caister. The local tradition has always been, that Caister was once the great city, and that the inhabitants migrated from it to Norwich; and such tradition is embodied in the old rhyme—a variety of one which occurs all over England—

> " Caister was a city when Norwich was none,
> And Norwich was built of Caister stone ; "

but as the same story is told of Rising and Lynn, and of other places, no very great reliance need be placed on it. Certain it is, that both localities were simultaneously occupied by the Romans, and as Norwich had a name which may have been British, while Caister was never known by other than its Roman-sounding name, the probabilities are rather that the legend is untrue.

Early pillaged by the Danes, Norwich was in their occupation in 870, and in 878 was the head-quarters of Guthrun, and to whom East Anglia had by way of compromise been allotted. Reverting to the Saxons for a long while, it again fell into Danish hands, when Sweyn sailed here on his errand of revenge in 1002, and is said to have burned the city. In 1017 Canute held it, and paid special attention to the Castle. Nothing of particular interest happened to the city till Ralph de Guaer's rebellion in 1075, when the Castle was stoutly but unsuccessfully held against the Conqueror. In 1094 Herbert de Lozinga moved the bishopric there from Thetford, and two years later laid the second stone of the Cathedral; and in 1137 happened the alleged murder by Jews of a boy, afterwards canonized as "St. William," for which many of that persecuted race were murdered. In 1216, the Dauphin's army, acting on behalf of the Barons and the Pope, plundered and burnt the town; and in 1234 was another persecution of the Jews, who this time were accused of circumcising a Christian child. The riot and burning of Jews' houses, which took place on this occasion, have been strangely confused by most of the local historians,* who erroneously ascribe to this date a riot between the monks and citizens, and a partial burning of the Convent—but nothing of the sort took place at this date. In 1272, the riot between the citizens and monks, which resulted in the partial destruction of the Convent, actually took place. It was caused in great part by the excessive arrogance and rapacity of the monks, and resulted most disastrously for both parties.

The most important epoch in the history of the city, was decidedly when the Flemish weavers settled here in great numbers about 1336, and gave an immense impetus to the industry of the place. In 1348—9, however, a frightful check to its prosperity was given by the plague, which is said to have killed one-third of its inhabitants. John le Litester's rebellion, in 1381, was another grave interruption to the growth of the city; but in 1403 it was thought important enough to receive a charter, giving it power to elect a Mayor and Sheriff. Disastrous fires in 1507 and 1509, owing to the great prevalence of the reed thatch; and the martyrdom of several reformers by Bishop Nix, in the reign of Henry VIII., were the most noticeable things which happened before Kett's rebellion, which took place in 1549. More martyrdoms in Queen Mary's reign were curiously enough the close precursors of the incursion in that of her sister of numerous Dutch and Walloon Protestants, of whom in 1582 there were close on 5000 in the city. One of them, Anthony Solen, was the first to introduce printing into the city, which he did in 1570. Queen Elizabeth paid a visit here in 1578, and was most royally entertained, but nothing of note took place for a long while; a great flood in 1614 being the only noticeable event. Taking but little part in the Civil War or the Restoration, the history of Norwich for the last 200 years has indeed been that of a prosperous manufacturing

* Blomefield, Goulburn, White, &c.

town, the inhabitants of which have been saved from stagnation by the exceeding bitterness with which all party and local political questions are discussed and contested, and by the hearty way into which all classes throw themselves into all really patriotic movements, when, *mirabile dictu*, their party feeling occasionally sleeps for a month or two.

" Hec est Norvycus, panis ordeus et halpeny pykys
Clausus porticus, domus Habrahæ, dyrt quoque vicus,
Flynt valles, rede thek, cunctantibus optima sunt hec.

Walk No. I.

Starting from the *Foundry Bridge*, which spans the Wensum just at the end of Thorpe Station Yard, we come at once into a new street, called Prince of Wales Road, which extends over what were once Spring Gardens and the site of the Friars Minors or Grey Friars—straight to the Cattle Market and the Castle.

Turning to the right when we get within sight of the Cattle Market, we come to *Tombland*, a wide open space in front of the Cathedral, which is thought by some to owe its name to being the site of some churchyard of a ruined ch., but which more probably means " toom " (empty or vacant) land.

The first thing to strike the visitor is the beautiful gate to the right (leading into the upper close) which is called the *Ethelbert Gate*—from the little ch. of that name inside the precincts, which was burnt in the riot of 1272. Its very fine wheel ornament in flint and stone panelling above the arch, is, though a modern restoration, specially worth notice. The older part of the gate has been shamefully neglected. It is generally said to have been built by the citizens to replace that burnt in 1272, during the riot between them and the monks, but it has been doubted whether anything of so early a date remains.

Between this and the *Erpingham Gate*, which is next to it, the wall has unluckily been built against from the outside, smugly respectable houses greatly spoiling the effect which a wall contemporaneous with the gates would have produced. One of the houses, however, has been recently removed.

Of the *Erpingham Gate* itself, which is the direct entrance to the W. front of the Cathedral, it is known that it must have been built by Sir Thomas Erpingham after 1411 (Harrod suggests 1420), for the arms of both his wives (Clopton and Walton) appear on it. A ridiculous statement has frequently found its way into print, that it was built by Sir Thomas as a penance for leaning towards Lollardism, and that the word 'pena' occurs frequently on it as evidence of this. The word actually is 'yenk,' variously read 'think' and 'thanks,' so the erection was rather in the nature of a thank-offering.

The lower part of the gate is richly covered with sculpture, the canopies especially being most beautifully carved. The buttresses are full of carvings of the arms of Erpingham, Clopton, and Walton, and are surmounted by two sitting figures of ecclesiastics. All the upper part of the gate is very plain, and seems unfinished, except that under a canopy is a kneeling figure of the builder, very finely carved.

Just inside the gate, and to the left, stands the official residence of the Head Master of the Norwich Grammar School, a picturesque building, grown over with a wealth of jasmine. Though almost every vestige of antiquity has disappeared from the exterior of the building, it is one of the oldest inhabited houses in England, and contains many traces of its original purpose, from which a reconstruction of its ancient plan might be made without much difficulty. It was erected by Bishop Salmon in 1319 as a *Collegium* for five priests, and subsequently increased to six, who were to serve the adjoining chapel of St. John the Evangelist together with the 'Carnary' (the crypt beneath), and say daily masses for the founder and his parents. The upper chapel, a very fine decorated building, with a beautiful piscina and grand windows, is now the Grammar School, while the 'Carnary' is used as the school gymnasium. In the latter were buried Sir John Wodehouse, in 1430, and his wife, whose skeletons were found entire in 1850, when the 'Carnary' was rescued from the ignoble use of a wine-cellar. Their tomb was at the same time desecrated and destroyed by the "restorers." The walls of the school-house are in some places 7 feet thick, and even the interior party walls are never less than 3. It has been sadly cut about and mutilated, but recently, under the diligent care of Dr. Jessopp, the late Head Master, a well-known and able antiquary, much has been done to reinstate it to its former condition.

On our right, is the grassy enclosure of the *Upper Close*, much used as a promenade, as the bands of the cavalry regiments here often play in it. It has a statue of Lord Nelson, not in the best taste; in fact, the execution is hardly more than decent.

A passage to the left leads to what was once the " Green Yard," where open air preaching took place as long ago as 1370, and perhaps earlier.

The *Cathedral* itself now stands before us, though much blocked up as to its base by *débris* and accumulations of earth. It was begun in 1096, and dedicated in 1101, by Bishop Herbert de Lozinga, whose memory has been cruelly treated by historians, who have even alleged his name meant " liar" or " flatterer," a libel now set at rest, I hope for ever, in an able paper, by Mr. Beloe of Lynn, who demonstrates ('Norf. Arch.,' vol. viii. p. 302), that " de Lozinga " simply means " of Lorraine."

The whole length is 407 feet, of which the nave takes up 204, and the transept is 178 feet, and the whole breadth, with the aisles, is 72 feet. The spire is 313 feet high.

The *West Front* is, like nearly all the Cathedral, Norman, but much added to, and is the worst part of the whole building, the immense perpendicular window (filled with poor stained glass to the memory of Bishop Stanley), seeming to overpower the rest of the front, which in its sides retains its Norman character.

Under the W. window is a main entrance, also perpendicular (about 1430). The whole front has been undergoing a tedious but hardly happy restoration. In the garden to the right are the ivy clad ruins of a building similar in character to that in the Bishop's garden, mentioned hereafter, which Dr. Jessopp conjectures, feasibly enough, was intended for a halting-place in processions.

Stepping down into the nave, the floor of which is lower than the outside of the Cathedral, the prejudice excited by the mean exterior vanishes ; the grand long Norman nave, with its massy pillars, at once attracting attention. The ninth on each side is specially noticeable for its fluted spiral work.

Nor can one fail to admire the beautiful stone vaulting, though it is much later, having been built by Bishop Lyhart between 1446 and 1472, replacing what was no doubt a flat Norman ceiling, as at Peterborough, remains of the mouldings of which appear along the clerestory.

The bosses on the roof are so numerous and so elaborately carved, that they have been made the subject of an expensive work by the present Dean, an attention they well merit. They represent a series of episodes from the Old and New Testaments, many being very interesting if irreverent and grotesque. The vergers have a framed looking-glass, in which the bosses can be seen by the visitor, without having to semi-dislocate his neck.

In the centre of the nave roof is a circular hole of considerable size, which Harrod surmises was intended as an opening through which the image of a white pigeon filled with incense was swung to and fro at Whitsuntide.

Between the 6th and 7th piers on the right is the table tomb of Chancellor Spencer, reaved of its brass, and between the next pair the very late Perpendicular monumental chapel of Bishop Nix (early 16th cent.).

On the next pier are traces of the newel of the staircase to the old pulpit, the carved stone sides of which remain.

Against the wall of the S. aisle is a somewhat tawdry illuminated monument to the Wodehouse family. Both aisles have Norman arcades, except where they have been cut away for monuments.

In the N. aisle is an extremely ugly stained glass window to the memory of the late Professor Smyth.

On the respond of the last arch on the right is a curious mural painting commemorating William Inglott, once organist of the Cathedral.

Passing round on either side of the choir screen (chiefly 1463),* on which was the altar of St. William, the Boy Martyr—(the piscina still remaining to the left of the door), and which is surmounted by an incongruously cased organ— we come to the N. and S. transepts, which are of the same height and style as the nave and choir, and are similarly covered with a later roof with Scriptural bosses. Above the choir is the massive tower, under and round which may be seen some of the best preserved Norman work in the kingdom, the lantern of the tower, with its fine arcades, being specially fine. The tower itself was repaired externally in 1856, the Norman work being replaced with new casing. Its ceiling, which is very lofty, is highly ornamented.

Entering the *Choir*, one is struck by its great length, and

* The upper part is modern, 1833.

by the worthy way the nave is continued, and we can judge of the beautiful effect that would be produced if the unhappy choir screen, interesting only from its age, could be removed.

The very richly carved oak stalls and *misereres* (so called) in the choir, deserve especial attention, and though many of their subjects are difficult to make out, it seems clear they were *not* intended, as Blomefield states, for ecclesiastical caricatures, but are more probably quaint reproductions from Bestiaries. An amusing instance of how antiquarians differ, may be taken from the fact that Mr. Hart describes one of them as the 'Prodigal Son feeding swine,' while Mr. Harrod, no doubt correctly, is of opinion it represents a woman striking a fox who is running away with a goose ! They are of dates varying from the end of the 14th to the middle of the 15th centuries, and form a most interesting series.

The roof here too is of Bishop Lyhart's work, but the Norman *clerestory* has been replaced by one of very fine Perpendicular, lit with four beautiful light windows, which are continued round the *apse* in such a way that little wall space intervenes between each window, thereby giving a wonderfully light and airy appearance to the apse.

As to the date of the present clerestory, there is much difference of opinion, some attributing it to 1480, and others to more than a century earlier.

Past the lectern, a brass eagle of some antiquity, is a slab without inscription, which, from its position, is supposed to mark the burial-place of Bishop Herbert, the founder.

To the right, between two of the pillars of the choir, is the white marble altar tomb of Bishop Goldwell (*circa* 1499), with a richly-carved recumbent figure.

Inside the altar rails note some very fine modern Italian mosaic flooring, a munificent gift of the present Dean, and behind a curtain is the most interesting original Bishop's throne.

Behind these monuments, and leading out of the S. aisle, is the Beauchamp, or rather Bauchun, chapel, now used as the Consistory Court. It has a fine shrine for an image, and some good roof bosses, but does not deserve the term of beautiful sometimes given it.

Continuing along the S. aisle, note next the broken but beautiful font which belonged to the now demolished ch. of *St. Mary in the Marsh,* the parishioners of which now use the adjoining chapel of St. Luke as their place of worship. It has representations of the Seven Sacraments and the Crucifixion, finely carved. In the chapel just named, avoid as much as possible a most atrociously ugly stone pulpit. The stained glass window is to Prof. Sedgwick.

After leaving the Beauchamp chapel, we turn to the left behind the throne, where recent restorations have exposed much interesting work.

The back of the screen-work next the aisle is ornamented with an arcade of interlacing arches, but the back of the centre arch has a plain Norman door, only opening into a recess under the throne. *Harrod* suggests that this may have been an opening to the Founder's Tomb, but *L'Estrange*, more feasibly, thinks it was only an arch to carry the throne.

Opposite this was the entrance to the *Lady Chapel*, which must have been a magnificent building, yet further adding to the great length of the Cathedral, but which is said to have been stripped of its leaden roof and otherwise dismantled during the Deanery of Dr. Gardiner, in Queen Elizabeth's time. Against the arch, which served as an entrance to the chapel, is the curiously painted wooden reredos, elaborately painted, gilt, and diapered, which has been removed from the Jesus Chapel, and is thought to be of late 14th century work. Here also is a facsimile of a mural painting now destroyed.

To the right we come to the *Jesus Chapel*, which is of very peculiar plan ; one circular building leading at its eastern end into a smaller building of the same shape.

Sufficient traces of colour and pattern were undoubtedly found on its walls, and of tile work on its floor, to justify the recent recolouring and tiling, but the general effect is tawdrily gawdy and painful to most spectators, however useful it may be to give us a correct idea of what the interior of a chapel looked like in mediæval times. Similar traces of colour are to be found over most of the cathedral, but it is to be hoped their reproduction will stop here. Here one notes with great distaste a hideous modern brass chandelier, but the sealed stone altar slab is particularly worthy of notice, being, it is supposed, the only one in this country which has the sepulchre containing relics apparently unopened.

Further on we come to a low stone vaulting of two bays of the Decorated period, carrying a gallery raised above the and inconvenient building, resembling nothing so much as the Old Hungerford Market at London.

Keeping up St. Giles's Street, we reach the *Norfolk Hotel*, one of the three chief inns of the city, but possessing no antiquarian feature, and passing several lanes (*i. a.*) Fisher's Lane, leading down the hill to the river, and Willow Lane (at the end of which is the Roman Catholic Chapel), come to the fine Perp. ch. of *St. Giles*, which stands on the highest ground in the City. Its lofty tower (120 feet high) is one of the most prominent landmarks of Norwich. The ch. has been recently and very judiciously restored, and the chancel, which was long destroyed, well replaced. Note the handsome clerestory, and the very lofty and bold tower arch, much in the style of that at Cromer. There are two good brasses which are well protected, as are the other slabs, by matting. The wooden roof and porch are interesting.

Returning into the Market Place, we keep along its lower side, which is known as the *Gentleman's Walk*, and which has many good and handsome shops.

The *Royal Hotel* (formerly the Angel) stands here, and is a very large and commodious house, by some preferred, on account of its superior position, to the *Maid's Head* or the *Norfolk*. It has a yard leading through or to the road still called "The Back of the Inns."

On the other side of the Market Place, and half hidden by a picturesque block of old houses, reminding one of a corner of some Flemish town, stands the magnificent, cruciform ch. of *St. Peter Mancroft* (Magna Croft, or Great Croft or field belonging to the Castle), by many thought the finest parish church in England.

Outside, note the splendidly ornamented Perp. tower, richly, and perhaps too richly, covered with carved work, which carries one of the best and sweetest peals of bells in the country, and remark the long light clerestory of 16 windows placed very closely together.

Inside, the very beautiful carved oak roof, with fanlike supports, is the most noticeable feature, though the slender graceful pillars of the nave, too, should not escape attention, nor the curious Perp. font-cover, nor the singular carved Jacobean, and book-case-like, South entrance.

The vestry is very peculiar, and floored with rude oak boards. It contains a very curious alabaster carving of Saints, which was found when digging a grave. There is a dated piece of tapestry (1573) of the Ascension, just outside the vestry. In this ch. were found, some years ago, many earthen jars, arranged in such a way that it has been supposed they were placed there to improve the acoustic properties of the ch.

Turning out of the Market Place into Rampant Horse Street, we come to nearly the last ch. of interest we need see, viz.

St. Stephens, which is one of the most interesting, if not the most interesting, in the City, with a very long clerestory of 16 windows, with some unusual stone panelling under it. Within the roof is splendidly carved, and very interesting. There are six very capital carved stools, and a curious vestry, quite coeval with the ch., with a massive oak-ribbed roof, and a carved oak chair.

We may, on returning *viâ* the Market Place and London Street, turn to the left out of the latter down Bedford Street—crooked but picturesque—till we come to an alley on the right, which brings us to the old *Bridewell*, a notable instance of the beautiful flint work for which the city is so renowned. The portion of it which abuts on St. Andrew's Churchyard is the best, the flints being there squared so beautifully that you can hardly get a knife-blade between them. It also has some fine late Decorated windows, and is said to have been built by Wm. Appleyard, Mayor in 1403.

The ch. of *St. Andrew*, which is opposite the Bridewell, is thought by some to be the second best ch. in the city. It certainly has a fine square flint tower, with a magnificent tower arch, and a clerestory with ranges of 11 very large windows. Note inside, the sedilia, and old stalls, and "misereres." Under the E. window, which abuts on the side street, and which is filled with poor tracery, are 14 interesting heraldic shields, and there are about seven more round the corner.

WALK No. II.

Starting again from the *Foundry Bridge*, which is just at the end of the Station Yard, perhaps the best way to see the City is to keep on the E. bank of the river, along which is a footpath, past the modern ch. of St. Matthew, Thorpe Hamlet, and the ferry known as Pulls or Sandlings Ferry. This ferry leads under a picturesque archway, over what was once the waterway to the Cathedral, to the Lower Close.

A little further down we come to *Bishop's Bridge* the only one of the old City bridges now standing, and which was erected in 1295. It is a strong low stone bridge of three semi-circular arches.

We should here cross the river, for the road straight on leads out of the town to Pockthorpe, where are the *Cavalry Barracks*, built 1791-3, and to the high ground above the city, once the camping ground of Kett in 1549.

Crossing the river, we get into *Bishopsgate Street*, and come on the right to the *Old Man's Hospital* (founded in 1249 by Bishop Suffield), to which is, practically speaking, annexed the ch. of St. Helen's, which has been divided into wards for the reception of the old men and women of the hospital. A portion of the nave is still used as a ch., and is (as is the tower) of good Perp. work. There are some interesting bosses in a groined vault of the S. transept. The S. door of the chancel is E. E., and earlier than the rest of it.

Straight on is the way to the *Cathedral* (already described), so turning to the right by the Hospital Lane, we pass the ch. of *St. Martin-at-Palace Gates* (otherwise *at-Plain*), a poor Perp. ch. with some long and short work at the two eastern angles of the chancel ; and turning back get into Tombland again. Note opposite, in the entrance of a cheese-seller's warehouse, two huge wooden figures of giants, said to have come from Sir Thomas Erpingham's house.

Turning sharp to the right out of Tombland, we keep straight on down Wensum Street till we come to the old inn now known as the *Maid's Head*, which stands on the site of the old Bishop's Palace, and is on the right-hand side. Here a visitor may well make his stay, for it is decidedly the most comfortable inn in the town, as may be imagined from the Bar mess patronizing it. The house is one of the very few old inns now remaining where the host takes a personal interest in his guests, and a better guide than Mr. Webster to the county, and especially to its fisheries, one cannot have. The house stands on great arched cellars, and is said to have an underground passage to the Cathedral, wherein, as rumour goes, live nuns were once bricked up. The enclosed 'bar' is of Jacobean carved oak-work, and the oldest I have ever seen. Exactly opposite the Maid's Head is the ch. of *St. Simon and St. Jude*, which.

save historically, it being one of the oldest in the City, is an uninteresting ch. outside, with an attenuated square flint tower, but has a curious piscina, with a small carved oak screen to it, and in the spandrels of the door leading to the vestry are curious carvings of fish, eels, &c., on one side, and a man rowing a boat on the other (no doubt St. Simon). There is a fine alabaster monument (now very dirty), to Sir J. Pettus.

Keeping round it past some old flint houses whose gardens run down to the river, you come to a very picturesque nook—a tree, and some old houses—one of which, the Briton's Arms, once said to be a nunnery, opens behind on the churchyard of *St. Peter-at-Hungate ;* the parish being so called because the Bishop's dogs were kept here. The ch. is small, Perp. Note a very interesting carving on the buttress of the N. door, dated 1460, of a young oak growing out of the bark of an old dead trunk, symbolizing the growth of the new ch. on the ruins of the old.

Opposite the side of the churchyard is the end of St. Andrew's Hall, nominally used by the Dutch congregation ; and turning into Princes' Street we come to the side of *St. Andrew's Hall* itself, which is a very splendid Perp. building, said by some to be built by Sir Thos. Erpingham about 1428, but others consider there is nothing earlier than 1450. It served as the nave of the Black Friars ch., the choir being afterwards given, as just mentioned, to the Dutch. When the dissolution of the monasteries took place, the city had a grant of it for a public hall, but it was greatly neglected till 1863, when it was restored at a very heavy expense. The propriety of the restoration was fiercely called to question, and two carved stone satires on Mr. Bacon, who unsuccessfully objected to the porch, and who was a distinguished musician, may be seen in the shape of a wide-mouthed hog swallowing a small model of the porch, and of a pig playing on an organ ; these being probably the latest specimens of this sort of caricature in England.

Below it, and nearer the river, stood the old monastery of the Black Friars.

Running along the end of St. Andrew's Hall is St. George's Street, crossing the river by *St. George's Bridge* to Colegate St., which runs parallel with the river, and in which are the small early Perp. churches of *St. Clement,* (with some good brasses and ch. plate, and in its churchyard a curious slab called the Leper's tomb,) and *St. George of Colegate,* which has a tall attenuated flint and stone tower, and a handsome flat timber roof. There is a very curious altar tomb to Robert Jannis, well worth notice ; and there is much good Queen Anne work in the panelling and pews. Here is the monument, with bust, to John Crome the artist. *St. Michael* (or St. Miles) *of Coslany*, a Perp. ch. with E. E. aisle, and, for a wonder, no clerestory. The last ch. is specially noticeable for the elaborate magnificence of its flint ornamentation. Especially note the delicate work of the aisles, and the imitation windows of stone filled in with flint panelling. There is some old glass, and a good peal of bells.

In Colegate Street, opposite to St. George's, too, one should not omit to notice that very interesting flint and stone house of *Henry Bacon*, Mayor in 1566. The door is in a fine state of preservation, and has his merchant mark, &c., in the spandrils. The upper story is of recent brick. On the other side of the way is a splendid red brick house with elaborately carved doorway and ornaments under eaves (Queen Anne), now in occupation of Mr. Corrick, and next to it is a doorway, dated 1570.

Turning back over St. George's Bridge, and resuming our route past St. Andrew's Hall, we walk up St. Andrew's Street, noting, on the left, a very old flint, brick, and timber house standing back down a courtyard now used as the Norfolk and Norwich Model School, and come to the Free *Library* and *Museum*. The latter was founded in 1824, and is open free from 10 to 4 on Mondays and Saturdays, but access can always be obtained by a subscriber's ticket, procurable at most places of resort in the City.

The collections of British and other birds, and especially the *raptores* (presented by Mr. J. H. Gurney), and of fossils, are extremely fine, and most worthy of inspection.

The Library was built in 1856-7, and is a plain, not to say ugly, building. It has most of the books belonging to the old City Library, which were handed over to it ; but the collection is unworthy of the city, which, however, has several other larger libraries.

The Museum is nearly on the site of the old palace of the Duke of Norfolk—which extended along the river, the bridge over which being still known as Duke's Palace Bridge. It was built in 1602, and was probably the most sumptuous building in England belonging to a subject—if indeed the Dukes who lived in it thought themselves subjects; for, when the Duke of Norfolk was charged by Queen Elizabeth with attempting to raise himself to the throne of Scotland by marrying Queen Mary, he is said to have answered, that while he was in his bowling-alley in Norwich he accounted himself as a king in Scotland.

It was destroyed by the then Duke of Norfolk, in a fit of petulance, at the end of the 17th century, because the Mayor would not allow his company of players to march into the town with trumpets sounding; and there is not a brick of it now to be seen.

In the crook of the two ways to the left, opposite the road leading to the Duke's Palace, stands the beautiful Perp. ch. of *St. John, Maddermarket*, noticeable for its absence of chancel, and its fine clerestory. The E. window is Decorated. Here are several fine brasses, wisely removed from the floor and possible obliteration, and placed against the walls. The modern altar-piece is very elaborate.

At the north side of the churchyard, leading out of the path which runs under the tower of the ch., note an old building with a low pointed arch, probably once used by some one connected with the ch. Continuing our N.W. passage, we come to "Charing Cross," and, taking the left of the two ways, notice on the left of the street some very fine bold carving of griffins, &c., over a shop.

The house to which this belonged stands back, and has another entrance from the churchyard of St. John, Maddermarket, which we have just passed. It is now used as a Roman Catholic Chapel, and is one of the most interesting specimens of domestic architecture in the city, and can be viewed at times by the courtesy of the resident priest. It used to be called the "Strangers Hall," is in part Perp., and has a very interesting later staircase. Up the first turning to our left is the ch. of St. Gregory, which is noticeable for its fine interior, two fine altar-cloths, some splendid communion plate, a "sanctuary" knocker, and the strange elevation of the altar, which is raised 5 steps, being erected over an archway forming a public thoroughfare from the ch. alley to Charing Cross.

Keeping along St. Benedict's Street, we pass successively the churches of *St. Lawrence*, splendid late Perp., with a lofty tower, a good timber roof, and a grand tower arch, but which shows to greater advantage from the lower ground on the other side. The clerestory is of 11 windows. There is an old carved oak door in the porch, and in the spandrils of the tower door are carvings of the Martyrdom of St. Edmund, &c.

St. Margaret, which we come to next, is a poor plain Perp. ch., but has a fine carved chest in the vestry; and *St. Swithin*, another small ch., partly Decorated, but with a Perp. clerestory and a good font.

All these churches are on the right of the road, on a low level, and all have back entrances on Heigham Street.

St. Benedict's, on the left of the road, is situate in an alley leading up to Pottergate Street, and is a small poor ch., with only one aisle, and a round tower with an octagonal top. The ch. has been cemented, which gives it a curious appearance.

Soon after we come to cross roads, the left of which is Grapes Hill, which slopes up rapidly from the river. Keeping up it we come to the top of *St. Giles's Street*, and the *Gaol*, which is a very plain, not to say hideous, one-story erection—with the tops of all its walls laid with two or three courses or tiers of loose bricks, to render the escape of prisoners more difficult. It was built in 1827.

To the left of the Gaol is *Unthank's Road*, one of the best neighbourhoods out of the city, several good new houses having been built there, and the situation being pleasant. On its right is the Baptist Chapel, a large airy and light stone building, not without some architectural pretensions.

Keeping straight on, we come to *Chapel Field*, at the northern extremity of which is the Volunteer Drill Hall, a large new and very plain flint and slate building.

Chapel Field Road—which runs outside and parallel with the old City wall, fragments of which, chiefly rebuilt, can be seen at intervals behind the houses. When the open part of Chapel Field is nearly passed, note a small round tower built out of the wall, and still fairly perfect; for this, and the piece of the wall, are the best examples now existing of what the old wall and its towers once were.

In Chapel Field once stood the Chapel of Our Lady in the Field, now demolished. The title has been assumed by a dissenting place of worship. Going up St. Stephen's Road there is no trace of the gate.

To the left is *Victoria Station*, consisting of plain and ugly sheds, built round an erection once used as a theatre and tea-garden. The station is only nominally used.

On your right is the *Norfolk and Norwich Hospital*, a commodious red brick and tiled old-fashioned edifice, now rebuilding, in an airy situation, looking over open country behind.

A little further the roads fork, that to the right leading to Newmarket, and that to the left to Ipswich. The Newmarket Road is wide and very pretty, and shaded by a fine avenue of trees. Along it are some of the best houses near Norwich, and the Cricket Ground, and the beautiful nurseries of Messrs. Daniels and Messrs. Ewing, the last-named being very picturesquely situate, and well worthy a visit, especially to rosarians.

In the crook of the roads there is a drinking fountain, given by Sir J. P. Boileau, Bart., in 1869, surmounted by a bronze group of a woman giving a child water. The ornamental brick-work at the top is elaborate and good, but the general effect of the whole erection is heavy, clumsy, and bad.

Returning to where St. Stephen's Gates once stood, we keep along down *St. Stephen's Street*. We should note, on the left, the interesting plaster ceiling in the house of Messrs. Barwell, who very judiciously, in rebuilding, preserved it at considerable trouble and great expense. Also equally note, on the right, the old inn, known as the " Boar's Head," the exterior of which is the oldest of any in the city.

When we come to Rampant Horse Street, a turn to the right brings us to All Saints' Green, and *All Saints' Ch.*, in which there is a very fine and rich Perp. font, with the figures of Four Apostles. This should by all means be inspected. The S. windows of the chancel are decorated.

A few steps further round the corner brings us to *St. John, Timberhill,* which stands commandingly at the end of *Ber Street*—one of the oldest and most considerable streets in the city—and which runs along the high ground above King Street and the river. The ch. is very interesting, the font being Norman, and there being much Decorated work.

On our left is the small ch. of *St. Michael-at-Thorn*, so called from a thorn tree which once grew in the church-yard. There is still one growing in it, but I doubt if it is the old one. The ch. has a Norman S. door, and a very small tower, which, as is most of the ch., is Perp.; while at the other end of Ber Street is *St. John-at-Sepulchre,* a Perp. ch., which has an interesting font, something like that at All Saints.

Passing along a little further, and turning to the left down Southgate Lane is St. Peter, Southgate (late Perp.). Further down, and past where the gates stood, is a very perfect piece of the town wall in the grounds of the "Wilderness," with a fine circular tower—standing high over the river.

Below this, in *Carrow Vale*, are the schools and cottages belonging to *Colman's Works*, which are immediately adjacent, on the banks of the river.

Carrow Bridge is a modern one, (toll, $\frac{1}{2}d$.,) and only leads over some very uninteresting and low-lying marsh land behind *Thorpe Station* into the Thorpe Road.

Without, therefore, crossing the bridge, we keep on the W. side of the river, and proceed along *King Street*, which lies parallel with Ber Street; though on lower ground, but still considerably higher than the river. Some of the most picturesque parts of the city are to be seen from this street, as you look down on the river, through the courtyards and passages of the old houses, into sleepy yards and curious gateways, supported by great old balks of timber.

Soon after entering the street you come to *St. Peter of Southgate*, on your left—an ugly late Perp. ch., with nothing worth notice in it.

Two or three hundred yards further and you come to *St. Etheldred*, an interesting though small ch., with a great deal of Norman work, and a circular tower, with a Perp. octagonal top.

Still further down the street, and still on its left, is *St. Julian's*, which is thought to be the oldest ch. in the city, its tower being considered Saxon. The walls are Norman, and there is some fair Perp. work.

To a student of architecture these two last churches are extremely interesting, containing, as they do, so many styles.

Meanwhile, the *Old Music House*, on your right, with its two fine 6-light windows, should especially be noted. It was once the residence of Chief Justice Coke. Nearly opposite is the interesting carved oak sign (on a beam above a door) of the "Prince's Head," now a shop.

Further down, note, on your right, a fine pointed stone

arch up the archway to the "Old Barge," with shields on its spandrils. Note the old hinges and the spy-hole in the massive door.

Still further down is the ch. of *St. Peter-per-Mountergate*, a lofty and light Perp. ch. with a good tower. Under the E. window is an original Perp. vestry. Straight on, past the back of the Post Office, late Harvey and Hudson's Bank, will bring us back to Tombland and the *Maid's Head*.

The three great factories in Norwich are those of Messrs. Colman, Messrs. Bullard, and Messrs. Barnard, Bishop, & Barnard. There are, of course, many others, such as Messrs. Haldinstein's shoe manufactory, Messrs. Hill and Underwood's Vinegar Works, and Messrs. Jarrold's Publishing Office, which may be termed a religious tract factory in itself, but the three now to be described are specially worth visiting for many reasons.

That of *Messrs. Colman*, at Carrow, is primarily for the manufacture of mustard, of which they make more than is made in all the rest of England, but their starch and " blue " businesses are nearly as large. What, however, makes these works (which employ over 2000 workmen, and which cover over 10 acres of ground) specially interesting, is, that on them is made nearly everything that can possibly be wanted for use in the factory itself. Enormous stacks of timber cover both sides of the river for hundreds of yards, waiting to be cut up by very fine steam-saws in a carpenter's " shop," which, though here but an accessory to the main business of the firm, is perhaps as large as any in England. Paper is wanted for wrappers, and therefore there is a paper-mill. Tin cans are needed to pack the mustard, and consequently there is a large tin-plate manufactory. There is much refuse from the crushed seeds, and to utilize this an oil-cake business is carried on within the walls. The rail runs right through the works, and into the Great Eastern system, by Trowse, and the number of trucks loaded and sent out daily is something amazing. There is a flour mill (the largest in the county), a cask-making shop, in which casks are entirely made by steam, by a patented process ; a dispensary, with a resident doctor ; and, in fact, the place is a complete town in itself. The buildings are nearly all new, and are (with the exception of the paper-mill) exceptionally clean and well ventilated, and the workmen themselves seem especially well and healthy. The processes of manufacture are themselves simple enough, consisting, as far as the mustard is concerned, of crushing in great iron mortars, by pestles worked by steam, and of sifting through silk sieves, but, as mentioned before, the chief interest in this factory is the way in which it is made self-supporting in all things, so as to be quite independent of any other manufactory for anything needed to send out the completed article. There are extensive schools, paid for by Mr. J. J. Colman, who is M.P. for the City, and who also supplies his numerous workmen with capital dinners, &c., on the works, at prices which cannot be remunerative, and for which one hopes he gets his reward in " another place." The works are so extensive that visitors cannot expect to be shown over all, or even much of them, as it would take up some hours of any *employé's* time to do so.

Messrs. Bullard's Brewery, though not so large as the works just described, nor employing as many hands, covers no less than seven acres, and is the largest and finest in the county. I am not aware that the process of brewing here differs materially from that of any other first-class house, that spares no pains to have all the latest improvements in machinery, at any cost, but the works are kept scrupulously clean, and are very extensive. The stables are very large and very fine, and would compare favourably for comfort with those of many a country gentleman, the cost of construction being, I am told, amply repaid the firm by the exceptionally good health the horses enjoy.

As at Colman's, there are here some fine steam-engines, which are used for every conceivable purpose. Two of the most interesting appliances in the building are automatic cask-lifters, which bring the barrels up and down from different levels, and an invention for washing the inside of casks by giving them an up and down as well as a sideways motion. The beer brewed here is uncommonly good, but, as is the case with the produce of all the other Norwich brewers, frequently suffers greatly when it gets into the hands of the retailers, many of whom are too clumsy or too fraudulent to sell it in good condition or unadulterated.

This firm will give facility to any one who has any reason, other than idle curiosity, for going over the works.

The iron foundry of *Messrs. Barnard, Bishop, & Barnard*, is situate next to Messrs. Bullard's brewery, just described, and is one of the most extensive in the Eastern

Counties, covering about 2¼ acres, with four-storied buildings. The firm employs about 400 workpeople, chiefly on piece-work, it being as yet happily uninterfered with by trades unions.

The marvellous delicacy and finish of the hammer work in the well-known Sandringham gates, exhibited in the 1851 exhibition, first drew public attention to the firm; but though they have still kept well to the front in wrought iron, they have since developed ornamental castings to a yet more extraordinary degree—the highly artistic fronts to their well-known "Slow Combustion" stoves being the most noticeable use to which such castings are put. Most minute castings are made, this branch of the business being superintended by a very able foundry foreman (A. W. Hawksworth), who, with the general foreman, Mr. Pye, will gladly explain the processes and show the workshops. One specialty invented by the former is a moulding-machine, by which sand moulds are manufactured from any pattern, drawn out by levers, under the face-plates, and ready to produce castings in two minutes.

Another instance of the foreman's ability is, that whole iron chairs, of elaborate and really beautiful honeysuckle pattern, are cast in one piece—a most difficult operation. Garden utensils, mowing machines, rollers, very easy spiral-seated chairs, and a thousand other things, are also made on the premises; wire netting of every size and breadth, up to 12 feet wide, being made by a most ingenious invention of the late Mr. Barnard. The specialty of the firm is, per-haps, the well-known "Slow Combustion," or Norwich stoves, of which very many thousands are turned out yearly, and some of which are extremely beautiful when fitted up with Minton's tiles, and reproductions of old-fashioned man-tel-pieces. The designs of all the articles manufactured are indeed extremely good, most of them being now by Mr. Alfred Barnard himself, and the influence of an artistically-educated mind over the whole business is most beneficial to it. To an ordinary visitor the most interesting thing on the works is the "cupola," or cylinder for melting the iron. The fire, which is made up about 3 P.M. daily, is intensified by steam-blasts from pipes running round the whole of its inside; so fierce is it, that it melts, like lead, the great heaps of broken and scrap-iron of all sorts which are thrown into it. It is very curious to look through the purple glass eye-holes, and see the drops of molten iron dropping, like clear white honey, from coal to coal as they gravitate to the bottom. The cupola itself is, I believe, an American invention, but it has been improved on by the firm, by the substitution of a drop-bottom, which pulls out and lets all the *scoriæ* fall through, and a water-tap being simultaneously turned on them, the rubbish can be cooled and removed before the workmen leave, the tedious and unpleasant work of raking out being thereby saved. Owing to Messrs. Barnard's being cramped for space, and the buildings having been erected from time to time, the works are inconvenient, and, in my opinion, unnecessarily dirty.

EXCURSIONS ROUND NORWICH.

There are two or three places near Norwich, which, as they do not fall within any of the excursions I have sketched out hereafter, I may note here as being very well worthy of attention.

The first is *Caister*, which stands on the little river Tas, three miles outside the City gates, the best way to it being over the Bishop's Bridge. The ch., which stands inside the Roman station, and is dedicated to the martyr St. Edmund, is uninteresting outside, except that it has some of the red Roman tile worked up in it, and is a curious mixture of E. Eng., Dec., and Perp. The font, however, is very fine Perp., and well worthy of attention.

The camp itself is most interesting, the walls enclosing an area of 35 acres, with an inner enclosure of 27 acres, and is the largest in England. The mound, on which the old wall stood, can be perfectly well traced, and fragments of the wall itself peep out here and there. At the side nearest Norwich, much of the mound has been recently dug away to show the wall, which is here perfect enough. Immense quantities of pottery, coins (from Nero downwards), and other remains have been found here, and many of them are in the possession of Mr. Fitch, a chemist, in Norwich Market Place, who is a diligent "collector." As the farmer who holds the land is much troubled with trespassers, any one wanting to go over the ruin should first ask permission at the farm-house.

At *Heigham*, which is only a few minutes' walk along the river, is a most interesting Elizabethan house, now known as the *Dolphin* Inn, in which Bishop Hall lived. There is the date 1587 above the door, and in the hall is some earlier work, viz. a Dec. piscina, with a crocketed canopy. Several of the rooms are well worth attention as specimens of the domestic architecture of the period. The garden slopes down to the river, and at its end is a pleasant and well-frequented bathing-place, the nearest to the city. In the ch. is a quaint monument, a gilt skeleton of the Bishop himself.

Hellesdon is interesting for its pretty situation, and its small Perp. ch., with double piscina, and low side windows with original shutter and ironwork. The aisle and N. doorway are Dec.

Costessey (commonly shortened into "Cossey") is about 4 miles N.W. of Norwich, and is noticeable chiefly for its very beautiful and extensive park, in which stands the Elizabethan seat of Lord Stafford, which has been in the Gerningham family since it was built by them in the reign of Elizabeth. A new mansion also of Tudor-work is still in course of erection. The pictures (by Holbein, Vandyke, and others) are extremely fine. The Roman Catholic Chapel annexed was designed by one of the family, and is a very beautiful building, containing much stained glass. Here long ministered the Very Rev. F. C. Husenbeth, D.D., the well-known antiquary ("F. C. H."). The parish ch. is a large decorated building with a fine screen.

TOURIST'S GUIDE

TO

NORFOLK.

———•———

INTRODUCTION.

NORFOLK, the home of the "North Folk," and so called in contradistinction to the adjoining county of Suffolk, once, without doubt, extended far more into the German Ocean than it now does. From the earliest times of which we have reliable records, and doubtless for ages before, the whole of its eastern and northern coasts have been gradually wasting away under the action of the sea, and the soil washed out to form the dangerous sands and banks which lie off its shores. The Dogger Bank itself, which stretches 354 miles from N. to S. from Scarborough towards Jutland, is supposed by some to consist of the ruin of much of this and the other eastern counties; and whether this be so or not, it is a matter of history that the villages of Whimpwell, Keswick, Shipden, and Eccles, have been entirely swallowed up. Speaking roughly, the rate at which the sea has always come in is about a foot every year, and as there is no formation along the coast strong enough to resist or even to stay the even sweep of the current round it, the easy curve of the shore is nowhere broken. Plain sailing and steering though it seems on a map, it is, owing to the shoals and banks just mentioned, unhappily the most dangerous coast round Great Britain, and nowhere is the wreck chart more closely dotted with the marks of loss and disaster than from Yarmouth to Cromer.

From E. to W. Norfolk measures 70, and from N. to S. 42 miles, having a seaboard of over 90 miles, and in size is the fourth English county, containing 1,247,753 acres, and yielding in area only to Yorkshire, Lincolnshire, and Devonshire, while in fertility it is the first, for nowhere else is the land so highly or so successfully farmed, which is the more creditable to its farmers, as the soil generally is very light and poor.

Speaking roughly, Norfolk is an oval-shaped, flat county, with very varied soil, and much heath and wood, bounded on the W. by many miles of most uninteresting marshes and levels, cut up by straight dykes, where the fens have been drained into dry land; on the N. and N.E. by a range of low but picturesque cliffs, broken, near Wells, by a stretch of saltmarsh; and on the S.E. by long low sandbanks, just, and only just, keeping out the sea from secluded fresh-water marshes, rank with vegetation, and as yet unspoiled by rectangular drainage.

The variety of the soil, and of the natural features of the county, is very noteworthy. Fuller, in his ' Worthies,' remarks: " All England may be carved out of Norfolk, not onely to the kind, but to the degree thereof. Here are Fens and Heaths, and Light and Deep, and Sand and Clay ground, and meadows and pasture, and arable and woods, and gen-erally woodless land, so grateful is this Shire* with the variety thereof."

There is still a large proportion of common and waste land, the return in 1877 showing that 12,869 acres are still left uncultivated, though an enormous quantity has been enclosed of late years. Much of what is left is rabbit warren. Of wood also there is a great deal left, viz. 44,251 acres, exclusive of 1534 acres of orchard. With so much wood, there is, of course, plenty of game; indeed a Norfolk manor is a by-word for excellence among sports-men; but the county is, among sportsmen, perhaps even better known for its water than its wood, for every wildfowler and fisherman has heard of the Norfolk " Broads "—the great series of inland freshwater lakes which, connected by sluggish and hardly navigable rivers —teem with fish and wild birds.

Before going into some little description of the place and its products, it may be as well to say a few words as to its people, and the remains we find of each successive race who held it,

Of the *Britons* and their traces here we really know little and find less. The piles of lake dwellings have indeed been said to have been found on the Broads by

* A native of Norfolk would scorn to call it a ' shire.' Inhabit-ants of the shires are looked upon here as an inferior race.

some, but the discovery has been discredited by others, who see in them only foundations of recent boat-houses. The British names of a few places, such as Lynn, still indeed remain, but it is now generally admitted that the fabulous histories told by monkish historians and repeated by early topographical writers, as to Gurguntius and other British kings, were evolved out of the vivid imaginations of such writers.

When we come to the *Romans*, however, we feel firm ground at once, for, south of Northumberland, there are few counties which possess a richer store of Roman antiquities than Norfolk. The splendid and perfect walled camp at Caister St. Edmunds, close to Norwich, which encloses an area of 35 acres, and those at Tasburgh (24 acres), Castle Acre (12 acres), Castle Rising (8 acres), Brancaster (8 acres), Buckenham, and Caister by Yarmouth, are all noteworthy of visits, while the Roman road, which runs in a bee-line for 40 miles across country to the station at Castle Acre, is very interesting. A curious kiln, undoubtedly Roman, was found not long ago at Hedenham, and another many years before at Caister by Norwich. Norwich itself, and not Winchester as is often supposed, was no doubt the Venta Icenorum of the Romans, and it should not be forgotten that one wildly ingenious antiquary contended that *Julius Cæsar* really landed in Britain at Cromer, a view he sustained with much perverse ingenuity.

Of the *Saxon* inhabitants of the county very slight visible remains still exist. Various earthworks, such as those at Weeting and Flitcham,* have been ascribed to them, but with no degree of certainty, and the towers of Tasburgh and South Lopham churches have been supposed to be Saxon, and part of the dormitory of Norwich Cathedral has been guessed to be the remains of an earlier edifice. The Rev. R. Hart has also plausibly conjectured, however, that many of the so-called 'Norman' churches may in reality belong to the Saxon period, and specifies St. Julian's, Norwich. The best traces, after all, of the Saxons in our county, are the very numerous placenames, the greater part of the dialect, and the many personal names which, more or less corrupted, have come down to us. It would be an endless task to try to trace all such Saxon names, but such as Aldrich and Eldridge (Ætheldred), Allard (Athelwald), Elmer (Ælmer), Elgar

* Those at Earsham are now completely destroyed.

(Ælgar), Elwin (Ailwin), Aldwin, Burt (Beohrt), Burn (Beorn), Cudbrid (Cuthbert), Brightwin, Coleman, Dybald, Folcard, Lovegar, Seward, and others, are easily recognizable.

Of the *Danes and Norsemen* actual traces are also very slight—an entrenched camp here and there ascribed to them with more or less probability, and one or two trifling weapons, &c., being all we have to show. The people themselves though, and the names they gave many places, are still here, for nowhere perhaps in England was there a denser settlement, and the Hundreds of E. and W. Flegg have not a village which does not bear a Danish name. Certainly 184 villages and towns (and in all probability over 200) in the county bear names given them by the Norsemen, many of which, *e. g.* Horning, Kirby, Horstead, &c., are absolutely identical with the names of places still in Denmark ; and very many of our commonest surnames are purely Danish, *e. g.* Thirkettle, Snelling, Grimmer, Hammond, Skalders, Abel, Bagge, Ball, Bugg, and Frost.*

The *Normans* have of course left many and permanent traces in the county, nearly all of which was parcelled out among them. Very few places, such as Hautboys (pronounced Hobbies), and Eccles, actually took their names from them, though many villages owe their second or distinctive name to some Norman proprietor, such as Framingham *Pigot*, Stow *Bardolph*, Saham *Tony*, and Swanton *Morley*. Many Norman names, too, have come down to us, for in the ' New Domesday ' of 1873 we find among the Norfolk holders persons named Malet, Warren, Rye (all of which three names occur in the Domesday of eight centuries before), Bainard, L'Estrange, Le Grys, Verley (Varley), and Gurney.

The architectural traces of the Normans in Norfolk are very numerous and very fine. The Cathedral at Norwich, with its magnificent tower, unique as to size in England, its nave, its transepts, and its apse, are probably the finest examples of *Norman* work in the country. Other, but of course not so fine, pieces of Bp. Herbert de Lozinga's work, are to be found at St. Margaret's, Lynn. He also founded St. Nicholas, Yarmouth, but nothing worth notice of his date now remains there. Other noticeable Norman work is to be seen—tower of S. Lopham, the S. door

* I have treated on the Danish settlements in Norfolk at length in the ' Norfolk Antiquarian Miscellany,' vol. i., p. 188, and the ' East Anglian Handbook,' 1879, p. 132.

and corbel course of Wimbotsham, the S. door of Thwayt, and the N. door of Hales. Very many churches, and especially in the E. division of the county, as at Wroxham, Clippesby, Haddiscoe, St Michael-at-Thorn, Norwich, and St. Julian, Norwich, have fine Norman doorways left, while the rest of the church has been modernized; and there are two or three others nearly all Norman, of which style I may specify Castle Rising as a most magnificent specimen. The W. front of the priory at Castle Acre is very fine Norman work, and should be specially visited; while Norwich Castle, Castle Rising, and Castle Acre are good specimens of Norman castellation, as is Winwall House at Wereham of their domestic architecture. One of the minor Canon's houses in the Close, at Norwich, is thought to be Norman.

I need hardly say that with so many churches as we still have, and with so much wealth as the county once had when it was the seat of the most important manufacture in England, very many fine examples of the different later styles of architecture are yet to be found here. Of *Transitional* work we have perhaps less than any other style, but there are good examples at Snoring, W. Walton, and Walsoken.

Of *Early English*, the great W. window at Yarmouth, the W. front at Binham, and the so-called Gateway in the Bishop's Garden at Norwich (but which no doubt was, as suggested by Dr. Jessopp, a halting-place for processions), are three as good examples as could be found.

There is much beautiful *Decorated* work in the county, notably at Cley, St. John's Maddermarket, Norwich, Hingham, Attleburgh, and Aylsham; but owing to the great fervour with which church restoration and building were carried on during the *Perpendicular* period, there is far more of this than of any other style. Some of it is very fine, and richly ornamented indeed, *e.g.* the towers of Cromer, and St. Peter Mancroft, Norwich. The splendid and unusually long clerestories of the latter church, of St. Stephen's, and of St. Andrew's Hall, all in Norwich, are features very worthy of notice. Nor should the fine tower of Sall Church, or the grand church of Terrington St. Clement, escape attention. Of special features of interest in Norfolk churches, I may point out the unusual number and beauty of the *Roodscreens* which still exist, though sometimes mutilated. That at Ranworth is the best known and deservedly so, but Fritton is very fine. A *font cover*, or canopy, at Trunch, is said by some to be unique, and there are many well-preserved *Rood Turrets* and staircases, some churches, as Cromer, having two ; while the *Brasses* throughout the county are exceptionally numerous and fine. The "Peacock," and other brasses, at Lynn, the Felbrigg brass, the Hasting's brass at Elsing, and the brasses at St. John Maddermarket, Norwich, are some of the best known, the first named being perhaps the finest in England. Unluckily, with one trifling exception, all the brasses have been stolen from Norwich Cathedral.

So much for the ecclesiastical remains of the Normans and their descendants in the county. The subsequent—though long apart—friendly invasions by the Flemish, and by the Dutch, and the Walloons, to which Norfolk owed nearly all its prosperity, though working an entire revolution in the trade of the place, hardly affected its architecture, though many think that the richness of the roodscreens and the elaborateness of the brasses point to an importation of foreign art. Possibly some of the domestic architecture at Norwich, and notably the quaint block of buildings which obscures St. Peter Mancroft, may be due to the taste of these refugees, and certainly much of the rich and expensive church decoration in and near the seats of the wool trade was paid for by them and their descendants. The village of Worstead gave its name to the well-known thread invented by them, and no doubt many of their surnames remain with us, but the only example I can call to mind is that of Leavins—a name borne still by a well-known and respected printer at Norwich.

What with the very strong Danish, and the still stronger Norman, settlements, the numerous incursions of Flemings in the reign of Henry I., and of Dutch and Walloons in the reign of Elizabeth, it would perhaps be difficult to find any county in England in which the population is of so mixed a breed as it is here.

The very great bulk of the land is in the hands of just over 10,000 holders, the remaining 16,000 holders having only 2468 acres between them. The greatest holders in the county now, are the Earl of Leicester of Holkham (43,024 acres), the Marquis Townshend of Raynham (18,129), the Marquis Cholmondeley of Houghton (16,995), the Rev. H. Evans Lombe of Bylaugh (13,832), Lord Hastings of Melton Constable (12,737), the Earl of Orford of Wolterton (12,341), Lord Walsingham of Merton (11,982), Lord Suffield of Gunton (11,828), Sir Thos. Hare of Stow

Bardolph (11,033), the Earl of Kimberley [Woodhouse] (10,800), and Anthony Hamond, Esq., of West Acre (10,039).

The oldest families now holding any large amount of land who have held it in the male line for any length of time are—

1. Lord Hastings, whose male ancestors were owners of Melton from the reign of Henry III. (1216—1272), and his female ancestors still earlier.

2. Kemp, who have held Gissing since 1324, and much earlier by female descent.

3. Marsham, who have held Stratton since 1350.

4. De Grey, who held Merton from the same year, and from the conquest by female descent.

5. Woodhouse, who held some land at Kimberley since 1378.

6. Berney, who held land at Reedham in 1389.

While Cholmondeley, Bedingfield, Wiggett (otherwise Bulwer), L'Estrange, and Howard, also hold property through female descents which have been for centuries in the possession of their ancestors.

As might be expected, the seats of many of such large proprietors are very fine. Speaking in an antiquarian and historical light, those of Mr. L'Estrange at Hunstanton, of the Wyndhams (now sold to a Mr. Ketton), at Felbrigg, of Lord Walsingham (de Grey) at Merton. of the Marchioness of Lothian at Blickling, of Lord Hastings at Melton Constable, of the Lord Stafford at Costessey, and of the Bedingfields at Oxburgh, are the most interesting. The four great "show-houses," viz. Holkham (Earl of Leicester), Houghton (Marquis Cholmondeley), Wolterton (Earl Orford), and Gunton (Lord Suffield), are all comparatively modern, though grand enough and mostly containing fine pictures and other works of art, and standing in beautiful parks.

Besides the great seats, there are very many interesting halls, manor houses, and smaller residences, such as Caister Castle by Yarmouth, Rainthorpe Hall, E. Barsham Hall and Middleton Tower ; in fact, there are few counties which possess so many interesting specimens of domestic architecture.

The feature which strikes a stranger most throughout Norfolk is the great use which is made of the flint which abounds nearly all over the county. It is, or rather was, (for the present work is greatly inferior to the old,) beautifully cut and squared, and most accurately laid together, forming work which it is almost impossible to destroy. Very fine specimens of it can be seen at the old Bridewell, the Guildhall, the Ethelbert Gate, and the Church of St. Michael at Costany, all at Norwich; in the tower of Cromer Church, and on the front of the Guildhall at Lynn.

So much for the landowners and their houses. I may now say something of the land itself, and how it is divided.

Its 740 or more parishes are comprised in 35 hundreds, of which 18 are in the Eastern and 15 in the Western Division. Those in the Eastern are Blofield, Clavering, Depwade, Diss, Earsham, N. and S. Erpingham, Eynesford, E. and W. Flegg, Forehoe, Happing, Henstead, Humbleyard, Loddon, Taverham, Tunstead, and Walsham. The Western contains Brothercross, Clackclose, Freebridge Lynn, Freebridge Marshland, Gallow, N. and S. Greenhoe, Grimshoe, Guiltcross, Holt, Launditch, Mitford, Shropham, Smithdon, and Weylond.

The Deaneries are 26 in number, viz. Blofield, Breckles, Brisley, Flegg, Holt, Ingworth, Lynn Norfolk, Lynn Marshland, Norwich, Sparham, Taverham, Thetford, Toftrees, and Walsingham, in the Archdeaconry of Norwich, and Brooke, Burnham, Cranwich, Depwade, Fincham, Hingham, Heacham, Humbleyard, Redenhall, Repps, Rockland, and Waxham.

The Parliamentary divisions are N. Norfolk (2), both Conservatives, S. Norfolk (divided), and W. Norfolk (2), both Conservatives, Norwich (2), both Liberals, King's Lynn (2), one Conservative and one Liberal. Thetford, Castle Rising, and Yarmouth also used to send two members to Parliament. The last was disfranchised for incurable corruption, a fate very narrowly escaped by Norwich.

Party feeling has always run very high in the county and city, and some of the most fiercely contested elections known, in which fortunes were wasted, have taken place for the former. One was in 1768, between Wodehouse and De Grey (Tory), and Astley and Coke (Whig), resulting in favour of Astley and De Grey. The Cokes are said to have spent a million pounds in electioneering, a fact which seems doubtful to those acquainted with the idiosyncracies of the family.

Of late years, unhappily, bribery has been very prevalent, both in the county and Norwich, and especially in Yarmouth, which has paid the penalty by being disfranchised. The extent to which party feeling and bribery still go, even in the municipal elections at Norwich, strikes an outsider as being very extraordinary, nearly as much being often spent in bribery and treating at one of the Ward elections as is spent at a Parliamentary election elsewhere. The Liberal and Conservative parties, especially in Norwich, still keep apart from social intercourse to a great extent, and it seems absolutely impossible for men of different politics to be even decently civil to one another within months of an election.

The county is well off for roads ; in fact, the earliest turnpike road in England was made here near Thetford in 1695,* and Charles II. is said to have remarked that Norfolk should be cut up into slips to make roads for the rest of England. Those in Marshland are especially level and good, the worst being along the northern coast.

Of water carriage, too, there is no lack either by sea or river, for the sea washes over 90 miles of its coast, and its eastern parts are served by the rivers running through the Broad District, and their numerous ramifications from Yarmouth up to Aylsham and N. Walsham, while the Yare runs up from Yarmouth till it joins the Wensum, which carries on the water traffic some way past Norwich. The extreme South is skirted by the Waveney, which accommodates Thetford and other towns before it runs into the sea in Suffolk by Lowestoft, but the West of the county is not very well off in this respect.

With railways the county is well accommodated. The Great Eastern, which was incorporated in 1862 by an amalgamation of the Eastern Counties, Norfolk, Newmarket, Eastern Union, East Anglian, Wells and Fakenham, and E. Suffolk lines, practically serves all parts of Norfolk. The latest, and by many much regretted, branch it has opened is between Norwich and Cromer, a line which has greatly interfered with the quiet and privacy of the latter place. There is also a light single line railway from Yarmouth through the Broad district by Ormesby, Hemsby, Martham, &c., which gives great facilities to the anglers and sportsmen who frequent it. This little line will probably be carried on to Aylsham, the only town of any size in the county which has no station.

For many years the want of punctuality and general bad management of the company were proverbial—(it was

* Another account states that the first turnpike road in England was from Hethersett to Frettlebridge, beyond Attleborough.

nothing unusual to be an hour late between London and Norwich)—and accidents were frequent; but since the terrible one at Thorpe, near Norwich, when two trains were sent out to meet one another on a single line, with disastrous effect, a change has taken place for the better, and the trains are now fairly punctual, though still very slow. The bad state of the permanent way is believed was long the excuse for this slowness, and, though this was partially remedied last year, I suppose that until the long-hoped-for day arrives when the line is handed over to the Great Northern, nothing better need be expected.

The trade done by the county is now of course nothing like what it did when worsted weaving was at its full, its best known production being, after all, a natural one, viz. the herrings caught at the Yarmouth fishery. Still there is a good deal yet done at Norwich in shawl weaving and other similar fabrics, and also in shoe and boot manufacture, and there are several well-known and extensive breweries and manufactories for agricultural implements all over the county. Colman's immense mustard and starch works, and Barnard and Bishop's iron foundry, both at Norwich, are very interesting, and descriptions of them will be found elsewhere. Yarmouth business is mostly confined to fishing, but Lynn seems getting a rather large import trade.

It is, of course, to agriculture that the great bulk of the inhabitants look for their living, and throughout the county good and high farming is the rule, not the exception.* Vast quantities of lean cattle are brought here from abroad, and from the "shires," to fatten, more especially to the salt marshes and the extreme E. and W. of the county; and at the annual cattle fair on Tombland and the Castle Hill at Norwich, held the day before Good Friday, perhaps the largest show of beasts and sheep in England can be seen out of London.

The GEOLOGY of Norfolk presents very many features of interest to the student from the great variety of strata exposed to view.

Of the *Oolitic* formation, the Kimmeridge Clay has been exposed in several places, especially at the W. of the county, especially at Hunstanton and Gaywood. It is said indeed to form the substratum of the whole of "Marsh Land," resting on sand.

* Here turnip culture became general in 1727, and dibbling wheat was here first instituted in 1774.

Coming next to the *Cretaceous*—for the Portland Stone is conspicuous only by its absence—we first come to (1) the Lower Green Sand, which may be seen overlying the Kimmeridge Clay at Hunstanton. There is a considerable outcrop of this formation north of Lynn, especially at Castle Rising, where its fine sand, and at Middleton, where its quarry of ' car '-stone, are very noticeable. At the latter place Ammonites are often found, and at Dersingham specimens of Nautilus Radiatus. Above the Lower Green Sand is (2) the Gault, which here is red, and crops up near to Newton and Sandringham. It may also be seen at Hunstanton, which, geologically speaking, is one of the most interesting places in the county. Many interesting fossils, and especially Belemnites and Ammonites, are found in it. Of (3) the Upper Green Sand, which is generally found next, there are but very slight traces, and we next come to (4) Chalk Marl, or Argillaceous Limestone, of which there is not much more. (5) The Lower Chalk, hard and flintless, averages 50 feet thick, and is much used for buildings. Nautilus, Ammonites, and remains of a Saurian have been found in it. (6) The Medial Upper Chalk, with flints, runs northerly from Thetford to Wells, and is said to form the chalk downs of the county—underlies (7) the Upper Chalk, with flints, which runs across the county more to the east, from Bungay to Cromer, where fragments of it are often seen on the beach. Very many molluscous remains are found in it.

The next formation is the *Eocene*, of which the London Clay was found 310 feet thick in sinking a well at Yarmouth, and the next is the *Newer Pliocene*, of which (1) the Norwich Crag is very interesting. It can be seen along the N. coast line from Weybourn to Trimingham, and also in the valleys of the Bure and Yare. Of the numerous and interesting remains of fossils found in it one may mention mastodon, elephant, hippopotamus, rhinoceros, stag, horse, wild cat, hyæna, fox, and leopard. It is, however, (2) the Forest Bed, which is best known to all Norfolk geologists. The Rev. John Gunn very aptly states of it, that —" The magnificence and profusion of the elephantine, cervine, and other mammalian remains, are such as to render this deposit one of the highest interest to geologists, and the bed itself, from the remarkable changes it has undergone, is scarcely less so. It consists of two materials—a blue argillaceous sand, which constitutes the soil in which the trees grow, and an indurated gravel, which, from the quantity of elephantine remains found in it, is called the Elephant Bed." It stretches for 50 miles along the coast, but is most marked at Sherringham, Runton, Cromer, and Trimingham. Magnificent specimens of elephants' tusks have been found along the cliffs, especially one at Runton, measuring 9ft. 7in. long by 2ft. 8in. in girth, which is supposed to have belonged to an animal at least 16 feet high. Rhinoceros, hippopotamus, bison, and other bones are also frequently found, but perhaps even more interesting are the remains of trees, such as fir, yew, alder, and oak, with hazel nuts, fern fronds, and other vegetable matter. A fine collection from this bed is to be found in the Norwich Museum. Above this are (3) the Laminated Beds, which introduce us to the *Glacial Series*, with (1) the Lower Boulder Clay, (2) the Stratified Clays, and (3) the Upper Boulder Clay, above which is the *Valley Formation*, in the gravels of which are found flint instruments, though but very rarely in Norfolk.

Coming to *Botany*, one need hardly say, that with such varied soil as we have in Norfolk very varied vegetation is only natural. Very many more than half the English flowering plants are to be found in it, for we have wood, freshwater marshes, saltwater flats, chalk hills, sandy plains, heathery commons—in fact, nearly every variety of soil a plant could desire. A full list of plants found up to 1864 will be found in an account of the flora of the county by the late Rev. George Munford, at pp. 70 — 101 of White's 'History of Norfolk' (Sheffield, 1864), a most comprehensive and valuable work, and to which I have been greatly indebted throughout this compilation. To the stranger botanist, the rare water-plants of the Broads, the sedges, the rushes, and the ferns, and especially *Osmunda regalis*, will perhaps be the best to which to devote his attention, though the range of hills along the N. coast is a favourite botanical hunting-ground. To the lovers of *Entomology*, probably no finer spot on which to collect can be imagined, the profusion of vegetation causing insects of all orders to abound. Now that the fens have been much drained, *C. dispar*—the beautiful large copper butterfly, which was once common in the N.W. parts—is very rare, even if it still exists ; but *P. machaon*, the grandest British butterfly, better known as the swallow-tail, is still abundant in the Broad district, where the rank vegetation, and the consequent abundance of rotting and decayed matter, are also most favourable to the *coleopterist*.

To *Ornithologists*, again, the county is very well known, more varieties of birds being found here than in any other English county, a fact attributable partly to the extended sea line, partly to the varied vegetation, and partly to the extreme quiet and seclusion of the marshes and Broads of its eastern parts. The great Bustard, once so plentiful here, is now utterly extinct, while the Ruff and Reeve is fast disappearing. Hawks, wild geese and ducks, and sea birds of all sorts, are very plentiful, while the trade in wild fowl killed by the decoys or shot is something considerable. Still more so is the business done in catching and selling the *Fish*, both off the coast, in the herring and other fisheries, and up the rivers and Broads. Pike, perch, and bream abound in the latter, or rather did abound, for a system of netting has unluckily prevailed of late, and the destruction of unsizeable fish is beginning to tell its tale.

Having said so much of the land and its products, I may be excused for referring to some of the *Worthies* it has produced, and they are by no means few. Norfolk men have always been known as very litigious—have been said to imbibe law at the plough's tail—to sue a neighbour because his horse looked over their hedge, so it is not to be wondered at that the county has produced several well-known lawyers.

The first of these, *Ralph de Hengham*, who was Chief Justice of the King's Bench, in 1274, was a native of Hingham, in this county. He is generally said to have been removed from his office in 18 Edward I., and fined 7000 marks for corruption, but Foss ('Judges of England,' p. 338,) doubts this on what seems reasonable grounds, and thinks the offence which led to his removal could not have been a very grievous one. It certainly was a long settled tradition that he was fined 800 marks* for having erased from the judgment roll a fine of 13*s.* 4*d.*, and substituting 6*s.* 8*d.* for it, in pity to a poor man; so, after all, he may have been more sinned against than sinning. There certainly was, however, much corruption among the Judges in the reign of Edward I., when a general clearance was made of the whole bench, except John de Metingham and Elias de Beckingham.

* The " clock " or bell tower at Westminster is said to have been erected with this fine.

Sir Edward Coke was of an old Norfolk family, and was born at Mileham, being himself the son of a lawyer of some note. Of his great legal ability, his coarse flattery to the king, and equally coarse brutality to the subjects, there is no occasion to speak here ; but in his age he seemed to change his nature somewhat for the better, and to him, at all events, Englishmen owe the Petition of Right. One of his descendants was created Earl of Leicester, a title which became extinct, but which was revived in this generation in favour of a Mr. Wenham Roberts, the sister's son of the last Earl.

Coke's great rival, *Bacon*, is generally considered a Suffolk man, having been the grandson of Robert Bacon, of Drinkston, in that county, but I am inclined to think that it will be proved some day he sprang from the Bacons of Baconsthorpe in Norfolk, a strong race, which had already produced John Bacon, the " Resolute Doctor," mentioned hereafter, and Friar Bacon, the greatest natural philosopher of the Middle Ages.

Lord Chancellor *Thurlow*, too, whose character bears many points of resemblance to Coke's, was another Norfolk man by descent, though born in Suffolk, his ancestors having been settled at Burnham Ulph.

The last legal luminary the county has produced—though far below his predecessors in ability—was deservedly popular. Of the Norfolk descent of *Lord Cranworth*, Robert Monsey Rolfe, of Hilborough, kinsman to Lord Nelson, and descendant of the celebrated Dr. Monsey, there can be no doubt.

Of WRITERS. *John Bacon*, the " Resolute Doctor," who died 1246, must have been a man long in advance of his age. He was of very short stature, so much so that his theological opponents jeeringly said of him—

" Scalpellum calami atramentum charta libellus "—

i. e. pile his pen-knife on his pen, and that on his ink-horn, a sheet of paper, and a book, and you have Bacon's height. Sceptics and doubters were his antipathy, and his studies were deep and profound, Fuller justly saying of him : " He groped after more light than he saw, saw more than he durst speak of, spake of more than he was thanked for by those of his superstitious order,* among whom neither before or after arose the like for Learning and

* The Carmelites of Blakeney.

Religion." Next perhaps to him in ability, as well as in date, comes *Skelton*, the Poet Laureate, who died in 1529, whose poems are not read as much as they should be, though there are few poems fuller of wild rollicking humour than his 'Tunning of Eleanor Rummyng,' or of pathetic tenderness than his 'Elegy on the Death of Philip Sparrow.'* Nor must we forget the *Earl of Surrey* and his sonnets, or *Sir Thomas Browne*, of Norwich, who died in 1682. The author of 'Enquiries into Vulgar Errors,' and 'Religio Medici,' was undoubtedly one of the most learned men of his age, as was his predecessor, the eccentric *Dr. Caius*, who founded Caius College, Cambridge, and was physician to Edward VI., Queen Mary, and Queen Elizabeth. Later on, Sir Roger *L'Estrange*, the cavalier pamphleteer; *Brady*, the historian; *Horace Walpole*, the dilettante scribbler, whose best work was his 'Historic Doubts;' Tom *Paine*, the atheist; Theodore *Hooke*; Mrs. *Opie*; and *Porson*, the drunkard and greatest Greek scholar of his day, who was son of the parish clerk of East Ruston; help to swell the list of Norfolk literary men, which, in the present time, has been worthily closed by Harriet *Martineau*, *Bulwer-Lytton*, and George *Borrow*, the "Rommany Rye," perhaps the best, if least understood of them all.

Among *Philanthropists* we have Mrs. Elizabeth *Fry*—a Miss Gurney by birth, *Fowell Buxton*, the great anti-slavery agitator, and Capt. *Manby*, the inventor of the well-known life-saving apparatus, which bears his name, and was well invented in a county which deplores so much murderous coast.

No county has had closer attention paid to its *Antiquities*. *Le Neve*, prince of genealogists; "Honest *Tom Martin*," the jovial historian, of Thetford; *Blomefield*, our county historian, to whose unrivalled industry we owe the splendid though still incomplete history of the county; *Kerrich*, the unwearied architectural antiquary; Sir *F. Palgrave*, *Forby*, the glossarian; and *Cotman*, the illustrator of brasses; are among the best known names: while, of late years, *Harrod*, whose sound and able contributions stand out among the weaker papers of his local contemporaries; and *L'Estrange*, whose recent deplorable end deprived the county of the man who knew more of its antiquities than any of his

---

* Shadwell, another Poet Laureate, but of a very low calibre, was of Weeting, and Cowper was of Norfolk descent, on his mother's side.

predecessors, go to make up a list not to be easily equalled by any other county.*

Of *Painters*, the "Norwich School," founded by old *Crome*, is well known; while, among *Musicians*, Dr. *Crotch* and *Hooke* are familiar names. *Browne*, the author of 'Religio Medici,' Sir *Astley Cooper*, and other well-known *Doctors*, have come out of the county; while *Kirby*, the entomologist, Dr. *Hooker*, *Smith*, and *Lindley*, the botanists, are among our natives. Very many well-known *Agriculturists* have, of course, lived in so well tilled a county, such as, in by-gone years, "Coke, of Norfolk," and in present days *Clare Sewell Read*, the latter of whom might also be classed (*sed longo intervallo*) among our county statesmen, *Windham* and *Walpole*. With *Merchants* and financiers Norfolk began well with Sir Thomas *Gresham*, the founder of the Royal Exchange, but cannot be said to have flourished lately, when we remember the disasters of the Gurneys and the Harveys in the banking world. Of naval heroes we have Sir Cloudesley *Shovell*, Sir Christopher *Minns*, and, best of all, Horatio *Nelson*, a name with which we may well wind up our list of Worthies.

The *dialect* spoken by the natives is quaint, and differs greatly from that of most of the rest of England, being rich in words not found elsewhere. It has been treated on at length by Forby, whose 'Glossary,' in 2 vols., has been supplemented by Spurdens; and of late years J. G. Nall has published a more voluminous and less indecently garrulous work. Perhaps the best shibboleths by which an East Anglian may be known are—(1) the omission of the terminal *s* in the third person singular of the present tense of any verb—*e. g.* a Norfolk man will always say, "He *sit* still," for "He sits still;" "The gate *hang* stiff," &c.; (2) the equally curious disuse of any word denoting house or habitation, as in the case, "Will you come to *mine*," (house understood); "I will look in at *yours*," and so on; and (3) the inability to pronounce "th"—*e. g.* three, through, &c., are always rendered "tree," "trew."

The Norfolk accent or emphasis is singular, a genuine

* Of minor lights, Munford, Dawson Turner an industrious collector, Dashwood a great genealogist, and Gurney may be mentioned; but the existing generation of antiquaries, with two or three exceptions, such as Carthew (whose 'History of Launditch' is beyond all praise) is very weak indeed, and the County Society is simply stagnating.

Norfolk man raising his voice towards the end of his sentences in a sing-song manner, reaching the climax of loudness or emphasis at the last word of the sentence if it is a monosyllable, the penultimate if a word of two, and the ante-penultimate if of three syllables, in each case lingering lovingly on such syllable ; *e. g.* " Have you got any *beer ?* " " 'Taint *like*ly ; " and, " Nothing makes me ill so soon as *cu*cumber."

Many of the names of localities are pronounced in a manner widely different to that in which they are spelt— *e. g.* Aselton for Aslacton, Hazeboro' for Happisburgh, Havaland for Heveringland, Taberham for Taverham, Corket for Caldicote, &c.

It may not here be out of place to note the extraordinary way in which natives of this county adhere to the custom of giving a child, for a Christian name, the surname of some relation, generally the maternal grandfather, or some quaint Biblical name. The strangest sounding results are often obtained, for the mere fact of both names being un-euphonious does not apparently in the least deter the godfathers and godmothers. Probably no one would believe that such names as those which I cite here from the ' Norfolk Poll Book ' of 1802, ever existed out of a novel, but they are literally cited from that work :—Cockle Cadywould, Haseleys Peascod, Royall Ringer, Porter Bringloe, Salem Goldsworth, Guyton Jollye, Briggs Race, Crisp Stoakham, Royal Watson, Neave Bullitaft, Rowing Brasnet, Pitchers Eburn, Isagrey Hedley, and Brunning Maddison. To show the fashion is not yet extinct I may also say that in the ' New Domesday ' of 1873, I find :—Christmas Bear, Nebuchadnezzar Carr, Bennator Chastney, Grimmer Cock, Kerenhappuck Cockett, Durrant Dutchman, Agas Goose, Taylor Phœnix, Zebulon Rouse, and Trafalgar Stokeley. A " Cardinal Wolsey " used to keep a wine and spirit vaults in Oak Street, Norwich, and there were two " Robinson Crusoes " at Lynn. It would be an endless task to note all the quaint and curious names one comes across in old records, but as some few of them may amuse my readers, I subjoin such as I have come across personally :—Goodheart, Hardy, Sincere, Turncoat, Dullman, Dearbought, Gathergood, Toogood, Goodcook, Piemaker, Freshbread, Whitebread, Hardbeans, Makehaste, Drawsword, Wagpoll, Greenhood, Smoothhead, Newcomein, Truelove, Makemaiden, and Rake,—all of which I found in the Court Rolls of Burnham. Elsewhere

I have seen:—Cokerhose, Loudchase, Buckskin, Barefoot, Proudfoot, Rightwit, Pig, Sandy, Shakelock, Lookdown, Shortfriend, Brokenhead, Spindleshank, Spurnwater, Ragorside, and Childfather.

So much for the everyday life and peculiarities of the inhabitants. Perhaps I may be allowed to finish my preface with some notes on the traditions and superstitions of the county.

Beginning with the traditions, there is a very interesting paper (at p. 209 of vol. i. of the Norfolk and Norwich Archæological Society's Original Papers), written by Sir Francis Palgrave, on the prophecies current in Norfolk about the time of Kett's Rebellion. From it and the authorities it quotes, we read, how the noblest prince in all Christendom shall go through Shropham Dale to Lopham Ward,* to be slain by the White Lion under the minster of Lopham. Also, how the Danish duke, backed by the king of Denmark and sixteen great lords, shall land on the north coast at Weybourne Stone, and being met by the Red Deer, the Heath Cock, the Hound, and the Harrow, shall fight such a battle between Weybourne and Branksbrim,† that from the latter to Cromer Bridge,‡ it shall run blood, and the Danish king shall be slain. But the Bear shall seize the prince at Clare Hall, and send him off a prisoner to Blanchflower,§ and drive his men into the sea, drowning twenty thousand of them without dint of sword.

Next is to come the French king, who, aided by a traitor mayor, shall be let in at Weybourne Hoop, but as to whose fate the seer unkindly leaves us in the dark.

It is curious to note how every one in olden time thought Weybourne Hoop was the key of the county. We still have an old rhyme,

> "He who would old England win,
> Must at Weybourne Hoop begin."

And besides being referred to twice in the above prophecies, it was a place very carefully looked after at the time of the Spanish Armada. Situate in an amphitheatre of hills, the water runs so deep right up to the shore of its little bay,

---

* Lopham I take to have been a sort of outpost to Kenninghall, where the Duke of Norfolk, the White Lion, lived. This prophecy probably related to some ambitious scheme of the Howards.

† Brancaster?

‡ I do not know where Cromer Bridge can be, unless it relates to Felbrigg.   § The old Norman name for Norwich Castle.

that ships can ride there almost as in a dock, and, barring Wells, is about the only place on the coast line where a good landing place could be found by a hostile enemy.

Among other floating traditions of the same class which still exist in the county, is one, that three kings shall meet on Mousehold Heath, and the proudest prince in Christendom be their subject; and the firm idea in the public mind, that Mousehold was fated to be the scene of great achievements, probably attracted many of the rustics to Kett's standard, when he raised it on that charmed spot; and when they were cut to pieces, these same rustics were, as it has been observed, the unconscious instruments of fulfilling other ways than they intended, the old prophecy, that the ' County Gnoffes ' should fill up the vale of Dussins Dale with slaughtered bodies.

Sometimes we hear fragments of Mother Shipton's prophecies. Still harping on the all-engrossing topic of coming battle, they tell how a wondrous Londoner, a miller by trade, with three thumbs on one hand, is to hold the three kings' horses in the battle which is to be fought on the Rackheath Stone Hill, on the Norwich Road, when the blood is to run so thickly as to clot by the wayside, till ravens carry it away, and when nearly every man shall be killed, and males shall be so rare, that girls, if they see one of the opposite sex, shall run screaming home to their mothers, "Lawk! mother! I have seen a man!"

One quaint quasi-prophecy is, " Blessed are they that live near Potter Heigham, and double blessed are they that live in it," which, for sublime bathos, equals, I think, anything I ever heard.

Of superstitions, those relating to ghosts are, of course, the most numerous; and many a well-authenticated ghost-story have I heard in years gone by, when I unluckily did not note them down. The most interesting, in an antiquarian point of view, are, the apparitions of the Shrieking Woman at Aylmerton, and of the phantom dog, ' Shuck,' mentioned hereafter.

The first is of a pale woman, with long hair, that runs from pit to pit, on Aylmerton Heath, looking wistfully into each, and shrieking and wringing her hands at each disappointment.

The 'Shrieking Pits,' as they are thence called, are thought to be the remains of British earthworks.

I do not know whether young Lord Dacre, who is said to

have been murdered at Thetford through the contrivance of his guardian, Sir Richard Fulmerston, about 1565, by the falling of a wooden horse, purposely rendered insecure, yet prances up and down on the ghost of a headless rocking-horse, but nothing is more firmly believed, than that Lady Ann Boleyn rides down the avenue of Blickling Park, once a year, with her bloody head in her lap, sitting in a hearse-like coach, drawn by four black headless horses, and attended by coachmen and attendants, who have, out of compliment to their mistress, also left their heads behind them. Nor, if rumour is to be believed, is her father more at rest than she, for Sir Thomas Boleyn is said to be obliged to cross forty bridges to avoid the torments of the Furies. He also is said to drive about like his daughter, in a coach and four with headless horses.

A carriage-and-four-ghost at Caistor Castle, drawn by headless horses, which yearly, at midnight, drives round the courtyard, and carries away some unearthly visitors; and in the West of Norfolk, another specimen of this curious apparition, which " on the anniversary of the death of the gentleman whose spectre he is supposed to be, his ghost-ship drives up to his old family mansion. The gateway is walled up, but what does that signify? He drives through the wall—carriage and horses and all—and is not seen again for a twelvemonth. He leaves, however, the traces of his visit behind him, for in the morning the stones of the wall through which he had driven overnight are found to be loosened and fallen, and though the wall is constantly repaired, yet the stones are as constantly loosened."

I have been told myself, how an old man, called Sam Baldwin, of Pulham Market, over sixty years ago, was going along the road from Pulham Market Green to Rushall, and how, while in Mill Lane, he heard a carriage and horses coming up fast behind him, and how he drew aside into the hedge to let them go by, and as the horses passed him, he noticed the coachman was headless, and how as he cracked his whip the fire flew.

There is yet another carriage-ghost, which frequents a large field at Great Melton, divided from the Yare by a plantation along which the old Norwich road ran. I re-print the account of it from page 3 of the 'Eastern Counties Collectanea: '

" Close to the edge of where the road is said to have run, is a deep pit or hole of water, locally reputed to be fathomless, and every night at midnight, and every day at noon, a carriage drawn by four horses, driven by headless coachmen and footmen, and containing four headless ladies in white, rises silently and dripping wet from the pool, flits stately and silently round the field, and sinks as quietly into the pool again.

"The rustics tell you that long long ago, a bridal party, driving along the Norwich road, were accidentally upset into the deep hole, and were never seen again. Strangely enough, the same story is told of fields near Bury St. Edmunds, and at Leigh in Dorsetshire."

Returning to traditions about holes, there is a tradition that King John's treasure lies hid on the left side of the road from Lynn to Long Sutton, about half-way between the two places, in a dark stagnant pool of water known by the name of "King John's Hole." Some treasure was said to have been dug up while draining the land on the banks of the pool ('Notes and Queries,' 2nd ser., vol. v. p. 268).

The story of the two brothers of Wickhampton, who tore one another's hearts out, and were turned to stone therefore, will be found in 'Notes and Queries,' 1st ser., vol. xii .p. 486.

Of ghost stories pure and simple, the best known, perhaps, is that of the "Grey Lady of Rainham," Lady Dorothy Walpole, who is reputed to have been forced to marry Lord Townsend in 1713, and who is said to walk up to the present time. The ghost at Blickling, too, is a well-known one, and other minor ghosts are referred to in the 'Eastern Counties Collectanea,' p. 3.

Ghost stories, however, there are in abundance all over the county. Tharston Hall, for example, is said to have a shut-up haunted room; old Parson Solley once bound a ghost in an oak tree (now down) at Stratton St. Mary; and the ghost of a suicide, named Lush, is said to haunt the place at Redenhall called "Lush Bush," from the willow bush said to have grown from the stake driven through the dead man's chest. The latest and best ghost story, however, is that told by the Rev. A. Jessopp, D.D., a few months ago in the *Athenœum*, where he described how, at dead of night, a tall priestlike figure sat at his elbow while he was reading alone in Mannington Hall.

Unluckily not very many of our ancestors' ghost stories have come down to us in detail. In the Gately Register there is a very circumstantial account of an apparition correctly prophesying a man's death, which will be found set out in

' Notes and Queries,' 2nd ser., vol. vi. p. 279 ; and we have equally curious details of the " Black Dog of Bungay," and the ruin he wrought in a thunderstorm in the year 1577, at pp. 268 and 314 of vol. iv. 2nd ser., of the same work.

This black dog naturally brings me to the Shuck Dog, the most curious of our local apparitions, as they are no doubt varieties of the same animal. The writer on the Bungay dog calls him, " the Divel in such a likeness," and the late Rev. E. S. Taylor derived Shuck himself from " Scucca—sceocca "—Satan—the devil. He is generally taken to be a large black dog, with great yellow eyes, and to carry death within the year to any one he meets. Sometimes he is a gigantic dog with a blazing eye in the centre of his forehead (Salhouse), and at others, somewhat inconsistently, as a headless dog, with great saucer eyes, and a white handkerchief tied over his head (!) The headless variety is said to cross Coltishall bridge nightly, but the better known species chiefly affect the sea coast between Beeston and Overstrand, where there is a lane called Shuck Lane. There is also a Shock's Lane at Sherringham (vide N. and Q., 3rd ser., vol. v. p. 237).

This curious apparition will no doubt remind my readers of the well-known " Mauthe Dog," which haunted Peel Castle in the Isle of Man ; and as that is a peculiarly Danish locality it seems to bear out the theory advocated by Mr. Taylor (ut supra), and by the Rev. W. Munford ('Local Names in Norfolk,' p. 150), that this is a Scandinavian fiend.

The belief in the existence of a kind of beneficent fairy, called Hyter Sprites, still exists, and the Jack of Lanterns, Lantern Jack, or Lantern Man, is still firmly believed in. He is said to object to any one carrying a lantern near him, and will sometimes follow the benighted traveller home, and light up his windows.

Another quasi-supernatural visitant in the Fens is a sudden whirlwind called " Roger's Blast," not lasting more than a quarter of an hour, which is not infrequent in the marshes near Wroxham, Woodbastwick, Horning, and South Walsham.

I have heard of a " dole stone," in Flegg Hundred, which was reputed to come down regularly from its hedgerow to drink at the nearest waters, just in the same way that the menhirs and dolmens of Brittany are said to come down to the nearest running water at midnight.

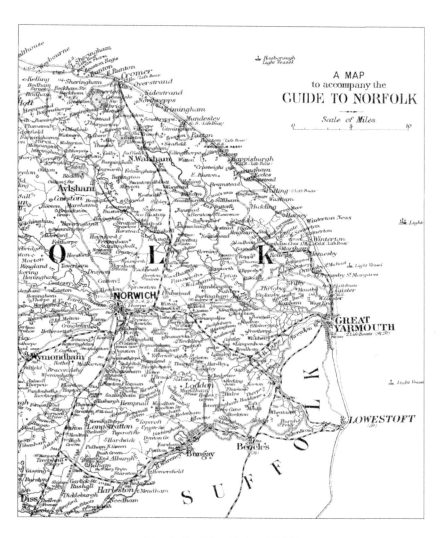

Norfolk (East) in 1880

Andrew Gill: I have collected historical photographs and optical antiques for over forty years. I am a professional 'magic lantern' showman presenting Victorian slide shows and giving talks on early optical entertainments for museums, festivals, special interest groups and universities. Please visit my website **'Magic Lantern World'** at www.magiclanternist.com

My booklets and photo albums are available from Amazon, simply search for the titles below. If you've enjoyed this book, please leave a review on Amazon, as good ratings are very important to independent authors. If you're disappointed, please let me know the reason, so that I can address the issue in future editions.

Historical travel guides
New York
Jersey in 1921
Norwich in 1880
Doon the Watter
Liverpool in 1886
Nottingham in 1899
Bournemouth in 1914
Great Yarmouth in 1880
Victorian Walks in Surrey
The Way We Were: Bath
A Victorian Visit to Brighton
The Way We Were: Lincoln
A Victorian Visit to Hastings
A Victorian Visit to Falmouth
Newcastle upon Tyne in 1903
Victorian and Edwardian York
The Way We Were: Llandudno
A Victorian Visit to North Devon
The Way We Were: Manchester
A Victorian Guide to Birmingham
Leeds through the Magic Lantern
An Edwardian Guide to Leicester
Victorian and Edwardian Bradford
Victorian and Edwardian Sheffield

The Way We Were: North Cornwall
A Victorian Visit to Fowey and Looe
A Victorian Visit to Peel, Isle of Man
Doncaster through the Magic Lantern
The Way We Were: The Lake District
Lechlade to Oxford by Canoe in 1875
Guernsey, Sark and Alderney in 1921
East Devon through the Magic Lantern
The River Thames from Source to Sea
A Victorian Visit to Ramsey, Isle of Man
A Victorian Visit to Douglas, Isle of Man
Victorian Totnes through the Magic Lantern
Victorian Whitby through the Magic Lantern
Victorian London through the Magic Lantern
St. Ives through the Victorian Magic Lantern
Victorian Torquay through the Magic Lantern
Victorian Glasgow through the Magic Lantern
The Way We Were: Wakefield and Dewsbury
The Way We Were: Hebden Bridge to Halifax
Victorian Blackpool through the Magic Lantern
Victorian Scarborough through the Magic Lantern
The Way We Were: Hull and the Surrounding Area
The Way We Were: Harrogate and Knaresborough
A Victorian Tour of North Wales: Rhyl to Llandudno
A Victorian Visit to Lewes and the surrounding area
The Isle of Man through the Victorian Magic Lantern
A Victorian Visit to Helston and the Lizard Peninsula
A Victorian Railway Journey from Plymouth to Padstow
A Victorian Visit to Barmouth and the Surrounding Area
The Way We Were: Holmfirth, Honley and Huddersfield
A Victorian Visit to Malton, Pickering and Castle Howard
A Victorian Visit to Eastbourne and the surrounding area
A Victorian Visit to Aberystwyth and the Surrounding Area
The Way We Were: Rotherham and the Surrounding Area
A Victorian Visit to Castletown, Port St. Mary and Port Erin
Penzance and Newlyn through the Victorian Magic Lantern
A Victorian Journey to Snowdonia, Caernarfon and Pwllheli
Victorian Brixham and Dartmouth through the Magic Lantern
Victorian Plymouth and Devonport through the Magic Lantern
A Victorian Tour of North Wales: Conwy to Caernarfon via Anglesey
Staithes, Runswick and Robin Hood's Bay through the Magic Lantern
Dawlish, Teignmouth and Newton Abbot through the Victorian Magic Lantern

Walking Books
Victorian Edinburgh Walks
Victorian Rossendale Walks
More Victorian Rossendale Walks
Victorian Walks on the Isle of Wight (Book 1)

Victorian Walks on the Isle of Wight (Book 2)
Victorian Rossendale Walks: The End of an Era

Other historical topics
The YMCA in the First World War
Sarah Jane's Victorian Tour of Scotland
The River Tyne through the Magic Lantern
The 1907 Wrench Cinematograph Catalogue
Victorian Street Life through the Magic Lantern
The First World War through the Magic Lantern
Ballyclare May Fair through the Victorian Magic Lantern
The Story of Burnley's Trams through the Magic Lantern
The Franco-British 'White City' London Exhibition of 1908
The 1907 Wrench 'Optical and Science Lanterns' Catalogue
The CWS Crumpsall Biscuit Factory through the Magic Lantern
How They Built the Forth Railway Bridge: A Victorian Magic Lantern Show

Historical photo albums (just photos)
The Way We Were: Suffolk
Norwich: The Way We Were
The Way We Were: Somerset
Fife through the Magic Lantern
York through the Magic Lantern
Rossendale: The Way We Were
The Way We Were: Cumberland
Burnley through the Magic Lantern
Oban to the Hebrides and St. Kilda
Tasmania through the Magic Lantern
Swaledale through the Magic Lantern
Llandudno through the Magic Lantern
Birmingham through the Magic Lantern
Penzance, Newlyn and the Isles of Scilly
Great Yarmouth through the Magic Lantern
Ancient Baalbec through the Magic Lantern
The Isle of Skye through the Magic Lantern
Ancient Palmyra through the Magic Lantern
The Kentish Coast from Whitstable to Hythe
New South Wales through the Magic Lantern
From Glasgow to Rothesay by Paddle Steamer
Victorian Childhood through the Magic Lantern
The Way We Were: Yorkshire Railway Stations
Southampton, Portsmouth and the Great Liners
Newcastle upon Tyne through the Magic Lantern
Egypt's Ancient Monuments through the Magic Lantern
The Way We Were: Birkenhead, Port Sunlight and the Wirral
Ancient Egypt, Baalbec and Palmyra through the Magic Lantern

Printed in Great Britain
by Amazon

35322101R00036

ISBN 9781533039590

90000

WHEN
RUNNING
IS NOT
ENOUGH

BECOME MORE THAN YOU EVER THOUGHT POSSIBLE

RAY FAUTEUX